THE NATIONAL POETRY SERIES *u*  *ie publication of five collections of poe* *ating publishers. The Series is funded ann* *rship, William Geoffrey Beattie, the Gettin*g*. *T*ami*ny Foundation, Bruce Gibney, HarperCollins Publishers, The Stephen and Tabitha King Foundation, Padma Lakshmi, Lannan Foundation, Newman's Own Foundation, Anna and Olafur Olafsson, Penguin Random House, the Poetry Foundation, Amy Tan and Louis DeMattei, Amor Towles, Elise and Steven Trulaske, and the National Poetry Series Board of Directors.*

THE NATIONAL POETRY SERIES WINNERS
OF THE 2021 OPEN COMPETITION

Symmetry of Fish
by Su Cho (Landcaster, PA)
Chosen by Paige Lewis for Penguin Books

Harbinger
by Shelley Puhak (Catonsville, Maryland)
Chosen by Nicole Sealey for Ecco

Extinction Theory
by Kien Lam (Los Angeles, CA)
Chosen by Kyle Dargan for University of Georgia Press

Ask the Brindled
by Noʻu Revilla (Pālolo, Hawaiʻi)
Chosen by Rick Barot for Milkweed Editions

Relinquenda
by Alexandra Lytton Regalado (Palmetto Bay, FL)
Chosen by Reginald Betts for Beacon Press

Ask the Brindled

Ask the Brindled

WINNER OF THE NATIONAL POETRY SERIES | SELECTED BY RICK BAROT

poems

Noʻu Revilla

MILKWEED EDITIONS

Published 2022 by Milkweed Editions
Printed in Canada
Cover design by Mary Austin Speaker
Cover photo by Jocelyn Ng
Author photo by Bryan Kamaoli Kuwada
22 23 24 25 26 5 4 3 2 1
First Edition

Library of Congress Cataloging-in-Publication Data

Names: Revilla, No'u, author. | Barot, Rick, 1969- editor.
Title: Ask the brindled : poems / No'u Revilla ; selected by Rick Barot.
Description: First edition. | Minneapolis, Minnesota : Milkweed Editions, 2022. | Series: The National Poetry Series | Summary: "Ask the Brindled, selected by Rick Barot as a winner of the 2021 National Poetry Series, bares everything that breaks between "seed" and "summit" of a life-the body, a people, their language. It is an intergenerational reclamation of the narratives foisted upon Indigenous and queer Hawaiians-and it does not let readers look away"-- Provided by publisher.
Identifiers: LCCN 2021062232 (print) | LCCN 2021062233 (ebook) | ISBN 9781639550005 (trade paperback ; acid-free paper) | ISBN 9781639550012 (ebook)
Subjects: LCGFT: Poetry.
Classification: LCC PS3618.E894 A92 2022 (print) | LCC PS3618.E894 (ebook) | DDC 811/.6--dc23/eng/20220105
LC record available at https://lccn.loc.gov/2021062232
LC ebook record available at https://lccn.loc.gov/2021062233

Milkweed Editions is committed to ecological stewardship. We strive to align our book production practices with this principle, and to reduce the impact of our operations in the environment. We are a member of the Green Press Initiative, a nonprofit coalition of publishers, manufacturers, and authors working to protect the world's endangered forests and conserve natural resources. *Ask the Brindled* was printed on acid-free 100% postconsumer-waste paper by Friesens Corporation.

for Haunani & my sly siblings
a me ka poʻe moʻo

Contents

III.

IV.

Ask the Brindled

I.

Definitions of moʻo

1. Shapeshifting water protector, lizard, woman, deity

2. Succession, series, especially a blood line

3. Story, tradition, legend

Maunakea

Inside me: two seeds.
One planted in my throat,

a dark highway
fingered by akua moonlight.

The other seed raised
in a fist of bright veins.

Who will taste without swallowing
my grove of lehua?

In a world terrified of rain,
who will kiss my kupukupu mouth?

‘O wai kou kupunahine?
I carry these seeds like a child

carries her grandmother's blood.
‘O ka ‘āina nō. ‘O ka ‘āina nō.

Trucks still carry medicine,
folding tables & hot food,

water   water
water   water

and the faithful still drive the dark
highway to ke ala hulu kupuna,

where the sky is so thin,
thinnest of all skins come to stitch

a new story, so thin I can still see bone.
From seed to summit, our bones matter.

'O wai kou kupunahine?
'O ka 'āina nō. 'O ka 'āina nō.

About the effects of shedding skin

Our grandmother speaks plainly. She lives in a small cottage in Hā'ō'ū, where Uncle B learned to climb coconut trees because *had to find food* and Aunty O didn't speak for days because *had to choose*. In Hā'ō'ū there is uphouse and downhouse. Relatives die in downhouse. Next to her bed grandmother hides her medical weed in an Altoids tin. Like her granddaughters, the joints we actually smoke come from town. The wine in our red Solo cups comes from town. The Costco tents, mosquito nets, deluxe coolers organized by meats and drinks. Only the rope comes from Hā'ō'ū. In plastic folding chairs, we listen to grandmother talk about shedding. And for the dark pit of her mouth, we have reverence. How she can stretch a no like a cobweb in her throat, and we stunned insects dangle. *Does it always hurt like this*, we ask. The black O her mouth makes tells us our land has changed forever. I remember a dream of grandmother's mouth snapping a yellow bird between her jaws. *Skin hurts.* Downhouse trembles. *What do you think happens after? You think skin stays skin just because it was skin to you?* Dangling, dangling. *What hurts? Show me where.* All the rope in Hā'ō'ū is waiting. *Show me.* Only ten fingers, where do we point? The hurt is origin story. And spreads. For some families, their evidence is blood. Our family, graves clean, our family is skin. *Stop scratching.* No longer children because we asked: Does it always hurt like this?

Welcome to the gut house

Outside a door in east Maui, a brindled dog sits.
        No cars drive the dirt road.
No child appears with food to share or ask for.
        There is only inside, today.
A telephone cries, and to each caller, a grandmother
        chirps, *Aloha. God bless you.*
In a corner bedroom, a girl is kept in bed,
        surrounded by mosquito nets & women
who take turns binding her wound.
        Miles of violence in their eyes, they know
how to speed through marrow. They know
        scars & stars, two things
a woman should never count in relation to her body.
        The number of names, maybe,
wired around her stomach. The number of stomachs
        opened like doors and not so much
cleaned as cleaned of secrets. Yes, there is something
        better than the heart. A whirring
sent deep in the body. Like a girl in a house.
        You are finally home.
No glorified organ, no heroic heart. Only guts.
        Viscera. Ask any Hawaiian.
Drive the dirt road, follow my grandmother's voice.
        She will bless you. My aunties & cousins,
their long fingers pinned to the walls, they point
        the way to a corner bedroom,
this poem. My sister is closing the mosquito net.
        I am pooling in a bed of gauze.
New versions of the Bible will use the word "heart."
        Ask any of us where it really hurts.
Even my grandma, god bless you.
        Ask the brindled dog guarding my stomach.

Eggs

There once was a girl with eggs in her eyes. *Hard shell, her.* They said she was really a lizard. *I saw her on my ceiling, once.* She was ten feet long. *I found her in my bathtub, once.* No bigger than a hand. Years passed and she never had a son. Years passed, never a daughter. Years of the island swelling with songs of a beautiful woman, *What a waste, what a waste.* Still, there were always whispers. Her eggs, her eggs. *Mālama pono ʻoe*, in hushed tones, *o lele ʻoe i ka pali.* She never bore children, but one day a trail of eggs snaked the village. Bones appeared. In their pots, in their pockets, in their mouths as they slept. Which came first— the girl or the lizard? Dream after dream of her splashing ponds. Out of shell, out of sight. Crack a lizard's eggs and you will fall off a cliff. What a waste, what a waste.

he mo'o
he mo'o
he wahine
he mo'o
he wahine
he mo'o
he wahine
he mo'o

is she family

he mo'o

he mo'o
he wahine

he wahine

he mo'o

he mo'o
he wahine
he mo'o
he wahine

he wahine
he mo'o
he
wahine
he mo'o

he mo'o
he wahine
he mo'o
he wahine
he mo'o
he wahine
he mo'o
he wahine
he mo'o
'he wahine
he mo'o
he mo'o

he mo'o
he wahine

he wahine

Survive,

he mo'o

he moʻo

is she

succession succession succession succession

he wahine   **is she**

fragment fragment fragment fragment frag
   is she

suc **is she gay straight** ssion succession success

fragment succession fragment succession

means she is fragment

succession fragment succession fragment

he wahine   **her survivng family**

fragment not fragment part of the whole

he moʻo
   he wahine

he moʻo   how did you survive

(s)he (s)he (s)he (s)he

(s)he (s)he (s)he (s)he

9

Kino

your black inscriptions cite a kino lau,

whose feathered wingspan, nighttime eyes & pun-

ishing beak comprise moʻokūʻauhau.

w/ my oiled hands, I greet her, w/ hun-

gering for moʻopuna. *mai*, she says,

reciting from your thigh. *mai, mai e ʻai.*

I have traveled from Maui a lizard, mes-

merized by dreams of ʻōhiʻa & ai-

kāne, lizard filled w/ smoke. arrived, I eat

transforming in the forest of your grand-

mother's memory: from lizard: woman

dreaming: licking tattoo: permission land:

skin. traveling the night of your kino

to sleep your thighs, hoʻāo, hoʻāo, and wake.

Mo‘olelo is the theory
for Hauwahine & Kahalakea

you splashed the water & flew the birds

vanishing before a different clan could follow you

    at Kawainui they stopped to disturb your lovemaking & lurk

      I'm still splashing water   still flying birds

        your descendent centuries later unseen unanswered

          we never asked them *watch us yes please swallow*

          us like water   we never splashed for them   even the birds

            know   where we vanish they can't follow

My grandma tells

me only some people have the eyes to see us. Shapeshifters fascinate, she said. And the ones without the eyes will clap & giggle, gazing only at our skins. How we shed & shed & never die. Reptiles, miraculous. But watch out, she tells me, dropping her wrinkled hands into her lap. The ones with the eyes. Sometimes they're worse. They know where you hide your tail. Duct-taped to your thigh, beneath your dress, throbbing. Only they can say I love you. They who see what happens at night when the dress comes off. They who see & do not run.

Memory as missionary position

I.
To fit a lizard, the jaw of this dress unlocks.
        Fitting sounds like eating, and mothers
                tell their daughter to shut their eyes.

Imagine *pins inside* the unmarried,
        pins to decorate
             the insides of a church.
        Girls wear dresses that mothers sew for them.

                            this dress //// flag //// shroud

In the 1800s my greatgreatgreatgreat grand
mothers swam to ships
to trade sex for cloth, iron, and mirrors.

Did you see yourself in their glass, mother?

Did you cut the shape of your body
        and send it whistling through the ocean?

                       When a cliff becomes altar

and the Pacific
in the name of civilization
is properly dressed

        daughters *inside*
             pine away

the altitude of faith.

II.
Inside the dress, there is a creature, she

careful

is a cliff in a girl's body.
And the cliff was a lizard once *still*   turned
to rock she gazed too much like she

careful

had a kingdom *inside.*

Inside the dress, holes are cut
    so the cliff can breathe and

        any girl watching
        any girl waiting
        any glint of a girl's

mother's metal scissors can *still* find her—

careful

there are still pins inside.

How to swallow a colonizer

after Kathleen Lynch with lines repeating from Haunani-Kay Trask

1. Brindle your throat.

2. Metabolize the twitching
    eyes, tongue, feet.

3. Hold your stomach
    with both hands while
    his teeth dissolve and recite:
    you will be undarkened
    you will be undarkened.
    This acid, medicine.

4. Always rub your piko.
    When the settler breaks down
    stick your finger in your mouth
    to beckon flowers.

5. Kaulana nā pua.

Catalogue of gossip, warnings & other talk of mo'o, aka an 'ōiwi abecedarian

I.

As long as my aunty's roofline.

Enough tail to wrap a truck.

In church, in traffic, in line at Liliha Bakery.

Only one I ever saw, only one I ever need to see.

Under the bridge. Look for yourself.

Her? Didn't look like a *her*.

Keep walking. Just keep walking.

Like nothing's wrong.

> Make no mistake.
>
> No matter who you are, who you
>
> pretend to be on dry land,
>
> when we get you, it is wet and honest.

'A'ole i pau.

II.

Another descendant may pretend not to notice

euphemisms in each conversation, the oh-so-sweet

invitation for my healing body to partake

of life after what-should-have-killed-you-but-

under-these-circumstances-keeps-you-wondering-anyway-

how-honorable-is-it-really-to-swim-upstream-with-your-mouth-open.

Kinder calls could not be made to help me be less

lonely. I remind everyone how daily it is to be broken.

Must the world suffer more creation stories?

Night gave birth to the lizard at rest, *so don't be so*

pleased with yourself, they tell me. A wasp's nest is growing

where my hurt should be.

'A'ole i pau.

III.

Antihero, someone suggests.

Expression of Native, feminist, and queer

in one body. Listen, there is never just one

or four, hundreds or thousands. Do you

understand what I mean when I say *swallowscape*?

How I eat one world at a time,

kick my pants off, brace myself

like a hurt animal on all fours.

Mean it—each time you fling your hips toward

night like bones to a monster.

Pick a better name for what you become

when you fly from my mouth, faster and harder than myth.

'A'ole i pau.

IV.
All lizards and shapeshifters, I belong to you.

Each leathery bundle born to protect water.

Incontestable genealogies. Drinkable. If there was

one question, one sagging wonder

untested . . . how hard did the others throw

her against the face of rocks?

Knowing her pain would be our pain—

leaves yellowing quickly—he kini ka moʻo.

Multitudes emerging not as replicas,

not as a museum of reptiles but reptiles in fact.

Pressed forever against the bones of her own breaking.

We who straddle to survive. From Kahoʻolawe to Mākena.

ʻAʻole i pau.

Don't have sex with gods

they hand me Bibles,
build church pews between my legs.
do your rosary.
do your rosary, baby.
but Father, forgive me—
I use my rosary as rope
the way Maui hauled the sun,
the way Maui hauled islands.

if ʻāina is that which feeds,
if aloha ʻāina is love and lover of land,
then she who feeds is she who fucks.
ʻĀina will fuck back.

what happens when the rope breaks?

do your rosary. don't do your rosary, baby.
we've always had sex with gods.

When you say "protestors" instead of "protectors"

I would call it a trick, if it wasn't so terrifying, how your mouth doesn't move when you speak. Your smile, shiny as a church, but what kind of prayer could ever be trusted without evidence of a free tongue? On the rare occasion sound shakes loose, words, no matter how unmuzzled, words still go to die. In your mouth, even womb is wound. Sometimes I dream of tearing your throat wide open and finding there, where stories should be born, only bleedingbleedingbleeding. The wish to desecrate. We are, yet again, portrayed by you, ~~the girl~~ ~~the Native~~ ~~the water~~ the mountain who was "asking for it." Your lips so Sunday still. Sometimes I almost believe you. So it's best I keep hiding knives in my hair, the way my grandmother—not god—the way my grandmother intended.

II.

Definitions of mo‘o

4. Narrow path

5. Small fragment, not attached to a larger piece

6. Ridge, as of a mountain

Iwi hilo means thigh bone

I have no prophecies.
My name is new &
narrow.   Without
question, I watch you
salt the corners of an
empty house in Pālolo,
chant the sky down until
it blackens & a star
becomes a spade in your
throat. 'Eli'eli kau mai.
You dislodge the metal
& tell me my fortune.
Tell me after whose
claw marks was I
named, still legible on
Maui cliffs. Tell me how
waters be damned, be
history. Or, tell me the
feel   of   it,   now.
Burrowing   so   deep
inside me until I was
never thigh bone & you
were always seed.

means core of one's being

Maui county fair

There were years I didn't attend the Maui county fair.
I blamed interisland travel, mind-numbing traffic
anywhere near war memorial park.
Too expensive, too busy, too old.
And yes, it's hard to hide from you.
I remember it fondly enough.
Hand in hand one year.
Watching each other across dirt
another year, strategic
beneath white entertainment tents.
Last year, my nephew said
he saw you and still calls you uncle.
Your new wife was friendly enough
even if she seemed nervous.
But I've seen you coupled and roaming
the fair grounds before.
The year I rode the zipper
three nights in a row.
Before and after poi doughnuts,
gripping the metal cage,
fingers wet with sugar and spit.
Returning again
and again to its mad tilt,
its fine spinning, the whole ship
of cages spinning up and down the sky.
It's hard to hide.
And that moment when your cage,
flung to the highest point,
spun to face the crowd as if this,
this is what you aim for—
hurtling toward the ground,
your face full of that Maui county fair.

In search of a different ending

I.   Summer with funeral & booze

It had been days since she found the bathtub selfies sent
to another woman. Always the same beginning: her
own skin peeling itself away, a cycle within a cycle, until
the day she decided to collect herself in glass jars. By her
own hands, build a structure of forgiveness. Forgive:
naked legs, lukewarm water. Forgive: tub they used to
fuck in.   *I wish I was kissing you instead.* As a child at
St. Anthony's church, she never learned to pray with
candles. Yet as a woman, she needed fire. Improvisation.
Display. Thinking she remembered a fact about god &
evidence—she ceremoniously labeled each jar. Here
was her skin, her faith. Like pages peeled from a hymnal.

II.   Summer with funeral & playing house

Are you in love with this one? The jars lining their bed-
room walls continue to preserve her skin. In her lap was
a jar for cigarettes. She sat near the bathroom window &
blew smoke at heaven, half-listening to the latest gospel,
half burning a hole in the sky: *she's just a* white picket
fence *she makes me feel* #skinoritdidnthappen *I didn't
mean* life after betrayal. She remembered St. Anthony.
Patron saint of lost things. Come, collect this body, saint.
I smoked you a hole to fall through.

III.   Summer with funeral & 3 a.m.

By the third lover, she had peeled so much skin she became a woman who could walk on blood. *She meant nothing to me.* She is a house of red. A holy assemblage. A city of nerve & dirt. *nothing to me* her skin survived every summer. *I don't want you to leave* she spoke to the jars. *I want you to live* like a city that never rises *live here* cigarettes *here* aimed at god. No evidence of life after death so she left that skin for good. Years later, she will remember the sound of her wife's tires flexing against mud, the sound of stolen glass jars ringing after her. By the third lover, she could finally walk on blood, but even the saint had gone looking for more skin.

Mercy

This morning I kissed a woman with a brick in her clay hands. *I am building a house*, she said. Brick in her hands, tongues in her mouth, door ajar. We kissed & I went searching for other bricks she brought this way, one by one in her clay hands. She smelled like a house, the one I saw built from scratch near the water tower in Waiʻehu. *Did you find more bricks?* I was young, a ten-gallon bucket clanging with nails. Who was I to say what was mine & not mine? *Did you find the water tower?* Over & over I searched. Bricks in hand. Ready to sleep in the roof of her mouth, ready to build a home and call her mine. *Did you find the door you tore open and ran from* mine *the door you buried in bricks* not mine *one by one* Waiʻehu torn *one by one* Waiʻehu built again? Memory made from scratch. *Did you find me there?* This morning I kissed each brick of this woman. Her name was mercy.

Ex is a verb

When the torch is more a crackling pit of
skulls & carrying it means Waikīkī
at two a.m., I love the pitiful
karaoke, pinkwash & standing room

only because we suffered together. Who said ex-
lovers shouldn't hook each other by the bra
& talk shit? Like which Venus woud be next
to make house & tangle with Gemini law?

Who with the horns, forward-thinking,
bright with faith, will grope in darkness
& make me a shape at last? Anything
but an edge to leap from, cliff incarnate.

We spent months sharing ghosts, our marrow mistaken for medicine.
But about this morning, you still haunt me. I still smell burning skin.

After she leaves you, femme

1. you will be a hole in the ground.
    a crater without glory,
    without science. in the ground
    you will forget we are the ones
    whose legs double as thunder.

2. tell me where it hurts, no one will say.
    leave land. leave sleep.
    walk to the ocean
    like your grandmother did
    when grandpa died.
    she just kept walking, aunty tells you.
    no slippa, not looking at anybody.

3. read audre lorde, cherríe moraga, haunani-kay trask,
    read warriors every night.

4. pile our legs like kiawe.
    let it be this skin, this form. if something has to burn.
    red flags we cackled and cut into skirts.
    maybe we are passage to the divine.
    & maybe we fuck ourselves in the shower.
    rub storm clouds alive.

5. wash your sheets   don't wash your sheets

6. in seven days, she destroyed your world.
    for the next seven, eat with your fingers
    & trust only the moon.
    there will be pressure-cooked pork.
    there will be gauze.

7. remember bare feet.
    remember the smell of ocean.

Lessons in quarantine

The second thing I learn is rain.
It falls harder here.
Like the woman at the end
of the road sleeps harder
& locks her doors at night.

Two years ago, with water,
digging stick & a mouthful
of seeds, I walked here.
To the edge of the city.
More mud, bark & branch.
Shades of brown, centuries in the making.
I walked here to live.
The third thing
I learn, this dirt.
This rain sent special for it.
This quelling of madness.
Everything will be green, again.

Yet the first thing,
the very first thing I learn is your hair.
Indomitable, wicked.
The first thing to pry my mouth open
& spit hard for.

So sacred, so queer

after Leanne Simpson after Billy-Ray Belcourt

so sacred

so queer

I learn **to grope**
for her

in dirt

so sacred
so queer

my
afterbirth
planted

our fingernails
before

so sacred

and after

so queer

so queer

I learned to bury

origin stories
that do not

want
me

in her
hands I learn
return is

so sacred

so sacred

a ceremony

when she
plants

my fingers

in dirt
she
makes

us feel
like
creation

so queer

so queer

fingering

creation
mai ka pō

mai
burials

protect
dirt
from
shame

we keep
the water
coming
so sacred
so queer
so queer

so sacred

35

Adze-shaped rain

Into a cave in Kalihi, two lovers vanished,

their bodies pressed against each other

they vanished

no ka hoʻopau ʻana i ke koena
o nā wahi i koe o ke kīhāpai
ʻaʻole i kanu ʻia

To seed instead of starve; be soil craving water.

Two lovers vanished inside a cave in Kalihi. Then the rain came to consummate

the
permission
to stay

not yet planted
not yet planted
not yet planted

In Kalihi, lovers keep sleeping as the rain falls sideways.

Days, nights.

nā wahi i i koe

nā wahi i i koe

nā wahi i i koe

Long before I was born, my kūpuna counted

three lovers instead of two. This work of sharpening heads:

the rain believing the ground believing the seed pressing deep

a single finger pointing the shape of Poʻolipilipi. Days, nights not yet

planted. In Kalihi, another story of desire.

III.

Erasure triptych

nvt. Food or food plant, especially vegetable food as distinguished from iʻa, meat or fleshy food; often ʻai refers specifically to poi; harvest (Oihk. 19.9); to eat, destroy or consume as by fire; to erode; to taste, bite, take a hook, grasp, hold on to; edible. *Fig.*, to rule, reign, or enjoy the privileges and exercise the responsibilities of rule, and one who does so, as ʻai ahupuaʻa: to rule an ahupuaʻa, the ruler of one; ʻai ʻaina: to own, control, and enjoy land; the owner of land; ʻai aliʻi, ʻai lani, and ʻai liʻi, to enjoy the comforts and honors and exercise the responsibilities of being a chief; ʻai ʻili: to control an ʻili land division, one who does control the ʻili; ʻai moku: to rule a district or island [moku], one who rules one. Cf. *ʻaialo, ʻai kanaka, ʻai nui, ʻai ʻokōa, ʻai paʻa, ʻai pala maunu, ʻai pilau, ʻai ʻuhaʻuha, ʻai waiū.* Various ways of eating may qualify ʻai, as ʻai, hele, ʻai lau, and ʻai noa, to eat freely and without observance of taboos (see also *ʻai kū*); ʻai kapu, to eat under taboo; ʻai kau, to feed by dropping poi directly from the fingers into the mouth, especially to feed a favorite child this way; ʻai maka, to eat raw; ʻai pau, to eat all. Hiki ke ʻai ʻia, edible. ʻAi ʻaha, to tie with sennit. Mōhai ʻai (Oihk. 2.14), cereal offering. Pāʻū ʻai kaua (For. 4:53), sarong worn in battle. ʻAʻohe kapu o kaʻu pā hula, he ʻai kū, he ʻai hele, there are no taboos in my hula troupe, eat standing, eat on the run. ʻAʻoheʻai ʻo ka maʻi, the disease makes no advance. Kāna ʻai, his food. Kona ʻai, his eating. hōʻai To feed, give food to, board. (PPN kai.)

2. n. Score, points in a game, stake, wager. ʻEhia ʻai e eo ai? How many points to win? (PPN kai.)

3. n. Dancing style or type. Cf. *ʻai ʻami, ʻai haʻa.*

4. n. Stroke or hold in lua fighting; spear thrust. Ka ʻai a ke kumu i koe iā ʻoukou (For. 5:409), the teacher's stroke that you do not have [have not been taught]. Kaʻai a ka uʻi, the stroke of the youth.

5. n. Stone used in the kimo game other than the stone that is tossed and caught, which is the pōhaku kimo.

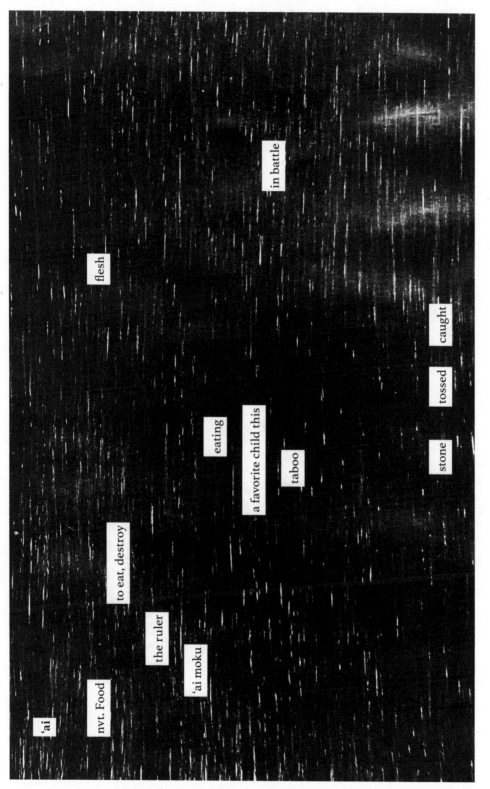

'ai

nvt. Food

the ruler

to eat, destroy

'ai moku

a favorite child this

eating

taboo

flesh

stone

tossed

caught

in battle

Notes on ʻai erasure

1. Draw boxes around words that resonate. Reveal obscenity. Reveal secrets.

2. How mesmerizing the back-and-forth of ink and fingers across the superfluous.

3. Erasure as anti-nuclear household.
    Pour black ink over the words you did not choose: **eat raw, hook, run, ahupuaʻa.**
    Remember: you are not making a home here.

4. Scratch, scratch, scratching.

5. **hold** Black it out.
    What did you just let go?
    What gave you permission?

6. Erasure poems require fortitude. Imagine a reader who will cherish this beast.

7. Your right hand going numb from all the 'ai.
   Destroy, eat, govern.
   The dictionary definition refers to land division.
   Suddenly your pen loses ink. This is no accident.

8. Black, black, blacking out.

9. You feel like church. Dazed not by the back-and-forth but by the muscles hot in your hand.
   Do you mean to call this thing destruction? Or creation?

10. The in-between spaces breathe better here.
    Trust the gaps like those in your cousin's front teeth.

11. Erasure poetry is not extractive   **flesh in battle**   this new ground has a name.
    Imagine a reader protecting this land.

Sirens   out

an Indigenous erasure of Annie Dillard

THE Tahitians are a beautiful languorous people devoted
to pleasure. That is how they were when the missionaries
found them, and that is how they are again today.

           It is so pleasure-seeking that this visitor, at
least, was struck with the comical thought that what these
islands need at this moment is more missionaries.

    Nothing more fully embodies this sense
than the *vahine*, the island women.

    Like flowers, they specialize in bright beauty,
passivity, and sexuality.

          Gauguin   girl
long pliant

   fifteen

her eyes roll back in her head

Where
well-nourished

tourists

thrive.

In 1772 Bougainville described the hospitality na-
tives extended to his shipmates. Tahitians invited strolling
sailors into their houses, fed them, and offered them their
daughters. Immediately the house would fill with curious
onlookers who surrounded the couple and spread the ground
with leaves and flowers. Musicians appeared and struck up
melodies on their nose-flutes.

In 1767
Tahitian woman

                                                          offering herself
           one long iron nail. In 1803

                                                          girls

six inches of water.

Each   a single, enormous black pearl

                    to have a *vahine*

                    whole and enormous

vahine

his mango,

his potatoes Anna, his

many years

vahine

skin

h   i   m

a silver platter

vahine

break   they

must pay

their eyes flash   their hips roll

tourists

sewn with nylon

thread

How I love to see these grandmothers
        wear missionary

                                        deep

pounding of   skin

                    great-granddaughters

                heads

split

nvt, nvs. Aloha, love, affection, compassion, mercy, sympathy, pity, kindness, sentiment, grace, charity; greeting, salutation, regards; sweetheart, lover, loved one; beloved, loving, kind, compassionate, charitable, lovable; to love, be fond of; to show kindness, mercy, pity, charity, affection; to venerate; to remember with affection; to greet, hail. Greetings! Hello! Good-by! Farewell! Alas! Alas! The common greetings follow: Aloha ʻoe, may you be loved or greeted, greetings (to one person). Aloha kāua, may there be friendship or love between us, greetings (to one person); dear Sir. Aloha kākou, same as above, but to more than one person. Ke aloha nō! Aloha! Greetings! (The nō may be prolonged for emphasis.) (Gram. 4.6) The following greetings were introduced after European times; Aloha ahiahi, good evening. Aloha kakahiaka, good morning. Cf. *aloha ʻāina, hanaaloha.* Aloha aliʻi, royalist, royal love. Aloha ʻino! What a pity! Alas! [Expression of regret, either great or small.] Aloha akua, love of god; divine love, pity, charity. Mea aloha, loved one, beloved. Aloha makua, considerate and thoughtful of parents and elders, filial. Aloha ʻia, beloved, pitied. Aloha pumehana, warm aloha, affection. Me ke aloha o Ka-wena, with the love (or greeting) of Ka-wena. ʻO wau iho nō me ke aloha, I remain, with very best regards. Aloha ʻoe, ē Maria, ua piha ʻoe i ka maikaʻi, hail, Mary, full of grace. Ē Maria hemolele, e aloha mai ʻoe iā mākou, Holy Mary, have mercy on us. Aloha aʻe ana mākou i ke ehu wāwae o ka lani (chant for Ka-lā-kaua), we remember fondly the footprints of the king. E aloha aku au i ka mea aʻu e manaʻo ai e aloha aku (Puk. 33.19), I show mercy tothose I want to show mercy to. Aloha nō ia mau lā o nā makahiki he kanalima i kūnewa akula! Affectionate [memories] of these days of fifty years past! hō.aloha Rare var. of hoʻālohaloha. Cf. *hoaloha.* (PPN ʻalofa.)

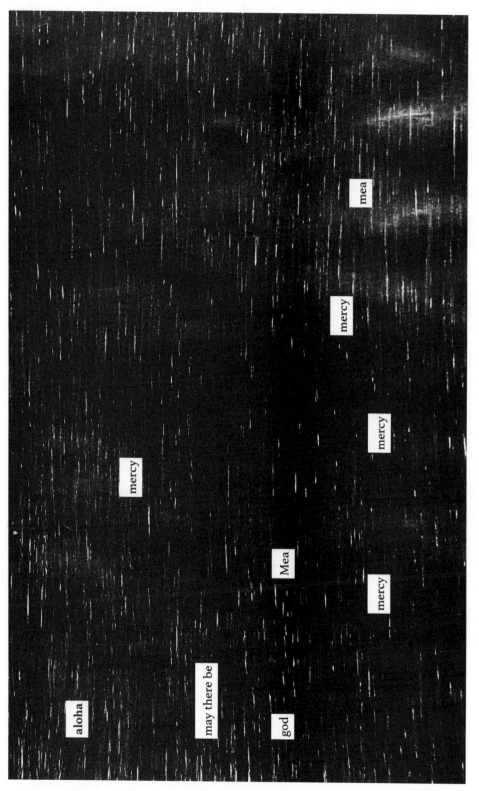

Notes on aloha erasure

1. Did you ever count the number of times aloha said *mercy*?

2. Of all the words with their hands open, why ~~love~~ ~~affections~~ ~~compassion~~ **mercy** ~~mercy~~ ~~sympathy~~ ~~pity~~ ~~kindness~~ ~~sentiment~~ ~~grace~~ ~~charity~~ ~~greeting~~ ~~salutation~~ ~~regards~~ ~~sweetheart~~ ~~lover~~ ~~loved one~~ ~~beloved~~ ~~loving~~ ~~kind~~ ~~compassionate~~ ~~charitable~~ ~~lovable~~ ~~to love~~ ~~to be fond of~~ ~~to show kindness~~ ~~to venerate~~ ~~to remember with~~ ~~affection~~ ~~to greet~~ ~~hail~~ ~~Greetings~~ ~~Hello~~ ~~Good-by~~ ~~Farewell~~ ~~Alas~~ Why keep crawling back to god?

3. Others offer brindled dogs, fat fish.
   In a cave in Hāʻōʻū my grandmother chews food with her mouth open,
   hangs skin that others have shed to dry on rocks.

4. Ua lawa mākou i ka pōhaku.

5. Yes, I have kissed mercy.

6. **I show mercy to those who come crawling to Kaʻuiki.**

7. nō may be prolonged
   nō may be pitied
   may hemolele have mercy on us

8. Damn it. The holy in me learned to swim. **Ke aloha nō!**

9. Erasure poetry builds family from scars, but forgiveness is not a home.

10. O kolo aku, o kolo mai
    I cross my forehead with grandmother's spit.
    O hoʻohua ka ohana o kolo
    and crawl where neither man nor god can enter.

IV.

Definitions of moʻo

7. Beloved grandchild

8. Brindled, of the skin, markings on those who feed and protect

Thirst traps

With the edge of a spoon, I scrape fish scales from my father's 'omilu & drop them into a Heineken bottle, nearly empty. My thumb is squeezed over the tiny glass mouth & I know if I choose to shake it, I must shake vigorously. The clump of scales needing the beer in the bottle, the beer in the bottle thinning the clump out, as if there never had been a body flopping on dry land before. I even know which cousin would drink it if I dare her. Because when we were young, girls could still keep their scales, could swim without drowning, hear tailgates grunt open & still glisten our bodies safely. But skins shed & skins later, we would emerge for any clapping fool, lunge even for mosquitoes. And skins lately, we've learned to drink our own storms, shaking for open water & calling it redemption.

A family poem.

Myth bitch

Before we stopped speaking, my mother told me of an all-woman island. *My side of the family*, she said, her mouth twisting like a sick branch. *And the women are witches*. I have since dreamed of women with heads of barbed wire. Torso in the bedroom, breasts in the sink. Legs divided between Oʻahu and Maui. Is *witch* the right word? When I sleep with a new woman, my mother whispers *fetus* into her fingers and sews my mouth shut. The fetus of a witch becomes a bitch. No daughter of hers will sleep like that. For the self-segmenting woman armed with needle and thread, rhyme is a mnemonic device. Repetition is rope. I will always look like my mother. Repeat: say nothing, daughter. Repeat: sleep alone, daughter. Daughter the word for *stitch her close*. When my blood touches her blood it means my mother is spitting needles. When I dream of women and wire it means I fuck like a woman at war with her body. Where is my rope? I am witch. I am island. Or am I a love story poorly translated? Fetus eating with a face to memorize. Mother, I am the myth bitch you dream about.

Getting ready for work

Public things:
  Lancôme powder foundation
  in a black case
  with a mirror.
  A row of pink tiles on the bathroom wall.
  Doorknobs.
  15 carpet stairs.

Private things:
  that I worshipped my mother's lipstick,
ate her nylons, and read the Bible for her.
I remember only that Eve is more evil than
the serpent so she sews prayers into my dresses.

          Mother often
          Mother make up
          Mother do mother do

  that I never imagined her as creature,
only mascara, Christmas
family newsletter face.

She had no mouth no mouth,

          Your mother had no mouth
          before she met me.

Private:

    his feet were Old Testament down
those stairs. Eyeliner can be surgery.
That black case died an oyster and the row
of pink tiles shit themselves. My mother continued.
    And her poor doorknobs.

          Child: eat   mother in public

For sisters who pray with fire

I love the smell of gasoline. My
sister loves fire. We keep memorizing her
list of objects to burn. The hot, devotional
theater of it all. No one will call
it fragrance, this service station blood
filling my head with firsts: the first

stick shift I knuckled white, the first
pack of cigarettes bought without my
passing magic. My sister, too, didn't bleed
but smoked. In a world raised without her
inflammatory hand, never called
or held, we teach ourselves devotion,

what it smellslike lookslike devoting
firetruck lungs. Fought that first
scratch of match and still they call
us emergency, us garland of risk. My
gasoline going everywhere. Her
theater filling with blood.

When I smell fire, she comes blood-
flecked and crackling, devoted
to each stick snapping through her.
First we aren't bright enough, first
we burn the suburbs down. My
sister's heart is a box of fuses. Call

her a good burn, call
us sisters in smoke. Blood
makes us radiant. Everywhere my
veins good at breathing us devout,
promising to love each other first.
Come what sulphur—my benzene her

Bic—come what may burn to watch her.
My umbilical cord, her umbilical
cord buried together. There is no first
without daughters. We are pre-contact blood.
Less discovery, less devoted
to the fire and brimstone. Bless my
sister for the guzzling effects of her
matchscape devotion. Her forever calling
my blood back. Back to what came first.

Dirtiest grand

we are the ones who know how to enter aunty v's house and choose a bed. we know Our Fathers are inevitably our uncles plucking us like 'opihi from fold-out tables. who were we before our skins bunched like salvation army skirts? or the moment smiling ruined our hips? we are the ones dreaming for tramp stamps, smoking menthols with our good-for-nothing mouths *but at least she can pack left-overs*. we're the ones in the dark with our tits out on kiawe trees. quick rinsing in the sink. confessing back and forth on earth as it is in heaven. forgive us. our ache to cling disappeared. forgive aunty p. the clink of after-hours jewelry. forgive the god of heinekens, the gods of piss corners & belts. knowing who got who without asking. are we the dirtiest grand daughters come to bless uncle's tarp? bluest tarp in Hāna. when the stink rises—because stink rises & never leaves—aunty v peels us out of bed like labels off beer, sends us not into temptation but the kitchen holding our own hair back. clean panties. cleaner sinks. anti-debutantes for spam and egg breakfast. while aunties flex a deck of cards for the first game of trumps that morning, we are the ones gently deciding who will sharpen the knives, who will chop onions, and who cleans the cutting board.

The opposite of dispossession is not possession; it is connection

yes there was

    loneliness

a story of

    loneliness was

three cousins and

    a rash

        fingernails so

they taught each other how

to grow

    long they could dangle

        fruit or children

so long still bone

they scratched and scratched naming

the reddest parts of each other

they chose the unloneliest words

even if they

    failed

like pa'akai or

lele one of them

born part cliff part

makani one of them

blowing the 'ōhi'a

    blooming inside another

an inheritance or curse

another kind of name

    was the rash

they couldn't say out loud

a tunnel of bone

    cracking

        scratching

centuries later

　　meant someone before them

　　　　could not bear

　　　　　　　less spirit

what they carried together

　　who was less bloody

made a thing

　　a thing to be nailed to

　　　　　nails

to be traded then

　　as strangers roamed drunk

　　　　on their skin

the rash spread

　　the t h r e e

　　　co u s i ns

　　　　　would

　　　　not resurrect

　　dead
　　　　　　dead
　　　　　　　　dead

　flowers
　　　flowers
　　　　　　flowers

The ea of enough

a story we must tell //// that we grew our daughters

in moonlight //// glistened their foreheads in salt

crown of bone //// etched in black //// daughters grown

to raise their heads /// to trust the songs of rupture

everything will fall /// you are shattered & many-named

believing no one knows /// how to call you home

home is a ravaged thing // we wish // you could see

the peace in the pieces / our bodies ungoverned by fear

we grew you in moonlight in the bone-flecked sky

the ea of enough is our daughters

the ea of enough is our daughters

our daughters need to believe they are enough

Fire in Mākena

What is your father's favorite fish, you asked.
I sat there ashamed, no answer to give.
My father is haunted, he will outlast
nicotine, meth, hyperthyroid. He'll outlive
MRSA, divorce, watching another
man with no home burn proof he
even exists. My father, I could tell you,
once, crouched behind a kiawe tree,
decided not to kill the man who set
what he had left on fire.
Why let him live? My father,
land locked in Mākena, simply said,
the difference between us was too small.

Recovery, Waikīkī

for Haunani

to the season without visitors, my single fin is another eulogy.
the sunscreen slick of queens is knifed by it and the cut remembers
somewhere deeper, somewhere far

$$\qquad\qquad\qquad\qquad far$$

$$\qquad before.\ the\ white\ procession$$
$$\qquad\qquad\qquad from\ here$$

$$\qquad\qquad could\ look\ like$$

$$\qquad\qquad\qquad white$$
$$\qquad\qquad\qquad wash$$

and we could believe, from far out here, the ocean was not
cauterizing a wound

$$\qquad\qquad again$$

$$\qquad\qquad\qquad we're\qquad drifting$$

for every street with an aliʻi name, ten thousand golden plovers.
funerals are everywhere. every time a tourist, whether warm or reckless,
every time a tourist, zero fucks given and helicopter rescue,
every time a tourist, whether cash or card,
every time a tourist says *lucky we* and *paradise,*
what if that stays in the air like dead skin
or drugs in a system that never disappears?

$$\qquad d \quad r \quad i \quad f \quad t \quad i \quad n \quad g \qquad we\ are\ wasting\ gods\ on\ this\ wave$$

to be this far out and learn nothing but how to count
ten thousand golden plovers backwards. this is bird shit before it dries.
it is waikīkī as covers of love songs

        (re)covering love songs i am (re)covering love
        as i paddle past a line
of dead bees, puffer fish, discarded lei in the ocean.

what sickness do they mean when the newspapers say that
                Waikīkī is "recovering" now?

            from the shore,
tourists must mistake us for brown water advisories, moving targets,
                a graveyeard-to-be.

            but my digging is dissent.

            before paddling this far out,
i dug ten thousand eel-sized holes into the groin facing the royal hawaiian.
i blew maʻi songs inside them.

        from ten thousand holes in the season without visitors,
        watch the Kumulipo re-emerge and take back Waikīkī.

New patient form—medical history—creative option

born to crawl and cling

at the edge of any

        thing : desire

                I thing where the cold
                gnarled concrete at Hāna Bay
                juts like a sore I thing it
                with my grandmother's toes
                ten tiny heads thinking out loud
                the bay, the only

List All the Bodies of Water That Came Before You All
the Bodies of Water We Will Become

thing : evidence

        this thing my grandmother
        and yes she really did climb
        all that way yes really she
        swooped her body like that
        thing my cousins and I do
        when the rope shows and one
        of us is tonguing the gap
        in her teeth smiling for
        the picture the picture
        always my mother snapping the surface

Things That Make Me Water Things That Make You
Blood All the Bodies We Have Climbed

thing : a keeping

> if you cut the rope deep enough
> our bones would show
> cut the picture open
> to hear the slaughter
> on a tin roof. *no cursing
> in my house*, aunty v
> would tell us. even if
> a cousin of a cousin took
> the ten minutes of walk
> armed with a knife
>
> : to arrive
> : to gut
> : the sky
> : swimming over
> : the house like a fish
>
> all of our women
> have that thing
> crawling inside us

List All the Bodies of Water that Came Before You All the Bodies of
Water We Will Become All the Things That Make Me Water Things
That Make You Blood All the Bodies We Have Climbed Out of All the
Water That Turned Against Us This is the Body This is the Blood

yes.

all of our women
have that thing
crawling inside us.

PUʻUHONUA : place of refuge

hookahi no kipi nui i koe
hookahi no kipi nui i koe
hookahi no kipi nui i koe
hookahi no kipi nui i koe

If they came to you, they lived.

o ko Aupuni **PROTECTED** in sacred & slaughter.

hookahi no kipi nui i koe
hookahi no kipi nui i koe
hookahi no kipi nui i koe
hookahi no kipi nui i koe
o ko Wahine

The penitent,

like kukui branches,

heaped at your ankles.

hookahi no kipi nui i koe **Can refuge** forgive refuge?
hookahi no kipi nui i koe
hookahi no kipi nui i koe
hookahi no kipi nui i koe
a nui ko malama i ko Wahine

Even your father
like water
warned

the danger of

canoes coming

a woman who

canoes becoming

hookahi no kipi nui i koe
hookahi no kipi nui i koe
hookahi no kipi nui i koe
hookahi no kipi nui i koe
paa ko Aupuni.

knows

canoes coming

she is more than omen.
Make battle formations
of your hips, Kaʻuiki

hookahi no kipi nui i koe
hookahi no kipi nui i koe
hookahi no kipi nui i koe
hookahi no kipi nui i koe
o ko Aupuni
o ko Wahine

Rip out your kuhina nui

heart. You are the favorite wife

of war.

a nui ko malama i ko Wahine

Basket

for Kathy Jetñil-Kijiner

She brings her host a basket:

> earrings, mats, testimony.

This basket, she says, *is medicine.*

> Some may ask: what is a basket to a bomb?
> Why bring medicine when they send ships   bombing
>   their laps
>   to jellyfish.

They didn't know what to call them, she said.
They didn't have a name.

> this ocean
>   an open wound

> but who gives a damn
>   moonlight scorched
>   from wombs
> who gives a damn
> who gives a damn
> who gets to damn who

> She brings her host a basket.

Then, bone by bone
    her low tide lips

> reveal the names
>   her gods & wayfinders
>   her mother & country
>   her island sea.

This is a basket of names,
a basket of stories.

For afterbirths
of fallout—

war-petalled

still sacred.

Shapeshifters banned, censored, or otherwise shit-listed, aka chosen family poem

The one whose maʻi was stolen as she slept.
The one who sold everything to live as bite marks.
The one named Mai, Mai, E ʻAi.
The one raising his scalp like foil from a pan of meat.
> *You know how many pigs I've killed*, he asks. And when he says
> *kill* he means it affectionately.
> Not *I killed pigs to feed my blood* but *I slept with pigs, my arms
> hooked around them.*
> When you love what you kill.

The one who thinks he knows who stole the maʻi.
The one with ʻōʻō feathers instead of hair.
> The years it took to catch each bird
> and adorn her head in yellow.

The one swallowing a kukui tree for the rest of her life.
The one who became the rest of her life.
The one still searching for the maʻi.
The one meant to be a locked door but fell in love with the crank of keys.
> *I'd rather hear that sound and die*, she said.
> Now all the doors in Kahului stay open.

The one made of open until her mother chased her with a knife.
> She is the cure to everything that hurts but will never
> let anyone touch her.

The one turned into long, solid sticks to poke women who, after kissing
> another woman for the first time, do not speak for days.
> In the grove in Hāʻōʻū, they plant their tongues.

The one who slept with the maʻi first.
The one who slept with the maʻi last.
The one currently sleeping with the maʻi because
> *maʻi was never stolen.*

The one all-remembering, coughing up cocounts as she laughs.
> Sometimes they call her grove. Sometimes, Hāʻōʻū.

Notes

Maunakea

In 1895, ʻŌiwi writer and newspaper editor Joseph Nāwahī asked two questions of the Kingdom of Hawaiʻi: *ʻO wai kou makuahine? (Who is your mother?) ʻO wai kou kupunawahine? (Who is your grandmother?)* The answer to both questions: *ʻO ka ʻāina nō! The land, indeed.*

Kanaka ʻŌiwi (Hawaiians) continue to protect their sacred lands and waters against desecration and extraction. Read Bryan Kamaoli Kuwada's *Ke Kaʻupu Hehi ʻAle* blog post, "We live in the future. Come join us."

Eggs

Remarking on the "terrible *moo* in Hawaiian dragon stories," Laura C. Green and Martha Warren Beckwith write: "'If you crush a lizard's egg you will fall off a precipice,' we used to say to each other. *Malama pono oe o lele oe i ka pali!* that is 'Take care, or you will jump off a cliff!'" See Laura C. Green and Martha Warren Beckwith, "Hawaiian Customs and Beliefs Relating Sickness and Death."

This poem is part of a longer practice of gratitude for Haunani-Kay Trask's poem "Sons," which was featured in her first book of poetry *Light in the Crevice Never Seen.*

He moʻo, he wahine

He moʻo, he wahine? Is she a moʻo or a wahine? "He" is an indefinite article in ʻōlelo Hawaiʻi, pronounced like the "he" in "hello."

Kino

Kino denotes the physical body. A feeling body is a thinking body, and whether I am shapeshifting through pain or pleasure, alienation or connectedness, I embody all the ways my ancestors have processed knowledge. By drawing parallels between the shapeshifting speaker and natural cylces of land formation, this sonnet participates in a tradition of Indigenous queer critique in Hawaiʻi that links aloha ʻāina and erotic sovereignty. ʻŌiwi scholar Noenoe Silva reminds us: "Our freedom to live in our land is linked to our freedom to determine how we live in our bodies, our freedom to live in relationships that may be different from American culture."

While a typical translation of *hoʻāo* is "marriage," the word is derived from *ao*, or "light." So *hoʻāo* can also mean "to sleep until daylight." The kahakō over the repeated word *hoʻāo* lengthens the experience of sleeping, dreaming, shapeshifting, or making decolonial love. In other words, when I say *hōʻao*, it does not mean we are married; it means we have spent creation together.

How to swallow a colonizer
The line "you will be undarkened" is the title of a poem by Haunani-Kay Trask.

In Hawaiʻi, "Kaulana Nā Pua" (Famous are the Flowers) is a beloved mele lāhui (song for the nation). Written by Ellen Kekoaohiwaikalani Wright Prendergast after the illegal overthrow of the Hawaiian Kingdom by American forces in 1893, the song expresses loyalty to Queen Liliʻuokalani and depicts the unified resistance of ʻŌiwi across our different islands.

Catalogue of gossip, warnings & other talk of moʻo, aka an ʻōiwi abecedarian
This poem draws inspiration from the Kumulipo, a Hawaiian cosmogonic record, specifically the fourth wā (genealogical era) that depicts the emergence of moʻo.

In the abecedarian form, the initial letters of each line when read down list the letters of the alphabet. The Hawaiian alphabet features five vowels (a, e, i, o, u) and eight consonants (h, k, l, m, n, p, w, ʻ). The ʻokina, or glottal stop, is considered to be a legitimate consonant sound.

'A'ole i pau is a well-known saying in 'ōlelo Hawai'i (Hawaiian language) often translated as "not finished." Used at the end of serialized excerpts of mo'olelo (historical accounts, legends, stories) published in the Hawaiian-language newspapers in the 19th century, this phrase signaled that more mo'olelo was in store for readers in the next issue. There were more than 10 different Hawaiian-language newspapers operating during this time, which produced more than 60,000 pages of articles, editorials, poetry, and mo'olelo in 'ōlelo Hawai'i.

When you say "protestors" instead of "protectors"
'O wai kou kupunahine? Who is your grandmother? And what does she teach you? Read alongside "Maunakea."

Iwi hilo means thigh bone means core of one's being
'Eli means "to dig" and its reduplication *'eli'eli* figuratively signals something firmly rooted or profound. The phrase *'eli'eli kau mai*, often said at the end of pule (prayer), is a spiritual request for a deepening of knowledge and/or connection.

So sacred, so queer
This title is based on Leanne Betasamosake Simpson's response to a line in Billy-Ray Belcourt's poem "sacred": "even though i know i am too queer to be sacred anymore, i dance that broken circle dance because i am still waiting for hands who want to hold mine too." To this line, Simpson writes: "I wanted to shout 'so queer, so sacred.'" Read Simpson's *As We Have Always Done* and *Islands of Decolonial Love*.

Adze-shaped rain
The rain of Kalihi on the island of O'ahu is named Po'olipilipi. In the story of the Po'olipilipi rain, two lovers stole away to a cave to make love. During sex, it started to rain, so the lovers remained in the cave to wait until the rain stopped. The lovers waited so long, they fell asleep.

In the Hawaiian-language version of the story, the metaphor of a garden is used to express sex: "ua peʻe ihola lāua ma laila no ka hoʻopau ʻana i ke koena o nā wahi i koe o ke kīhāpai ʻaʻole i kanu ʻia (And they hid in a cave until they could finish off the remaining areas of the garden that had not been planted)." In this poem, the Poʻolipilipi rain is an active lover. See Collette Leimomi Akana and Kiele Gonzalez, *Hānau Ka Ua: Hawaiian Rain Names*.

Sirens   out
This poem is an erasure of Annie Dillard's racist travel essay "Sirens of the South Seas."

aloha
The fourth wā of the Kumulipo documents the birth of reptiles, including moʻo. In the first paukū (stanza) of the fourth wā, kolo (crawling) is the primary kinesthetic imagery attributed to reptiles: "O kolo aku, o kolo mai / O hoʻohua ka ohana o kolo." Rubellite Kawena Johnson translates: "Where they crawl away and crawl here, / Family of crawlers increasing their kind." See Rubellite Kawena Johnson, *Essays in Hawaiian Literature*.

The opposite of dispossession is not possession; it is connection
This title is taken from Leanne Betasamosake Simpson's *As We Have Always Done: Indigenous Freedom Through Radical Resistance*. In chapter ten "'I See Your Light': Reciprocal Recognition and Generative Refusal," Simpson discusses the value of reciprocal recognition, which she argues:

> cognitively reverses the violence of dispossession because
> what is the opposite of dispossession? Not possession,
> because we're not supposed to be capitalists, but connection,
> a coded layering of intimate interconnection and
> interdependence that creates a complicated algorithmic
> network of presence, reciprocity, consent, and freedom.

The ea of enough

In ʻōlelo Hawaiʻi, *ea* denotes sovereignty, breath, and rising. Read David Kahalemaile's speech reprinted in the August 12, 1871 issue of *Ka Nupepa Kuokoa*:

> Ke ea o ka iʻa, he wai.
> Ke ea o ke kanaka, he makani.
> Ke ea o ka honua, he kanaka.
> Ke ea o ka moku, he hoeuli.
> ʻO ke ea o ko Hawaiʻi Pae ʻĀina,
> ʻo ia nō ka noho aupuni ʻana.

> The ea of fish is water.
> The ea of the person is wind.
> The ea of the earth is the person.
> The ea of the ship is the steering paddle.
> And the ea of the Hawaiian Islands
> is our independent governance.

Recovery, Waikīkī

The Kumulipo is a Native Hawaiian cosmogonic chant that records the origins of life in the natural world as well as the emergence of humans. In ʻŌiwi culture, the Kumulipo is a significant source of genealogical information, shaping what Noenoe Silva describes as "moʻokūʻauhau consciousness."

Preparing Kaʻuiki

This poem commemorates Kaʻahumanu, a political strategist, aloha ʻāina, and leader in a time of great transformation in Hawaiʻi. Born in Mapuwena, Kaʻuiki, Hāna in 1768, Kaʻahumanu was one of the highest-ranking aliʻi in Hawaiian history. During the time of Kamehameha Nui, her body and her lands were deemed puʻuhonua. In other words, her body and her lands were places of refuge for those seeking pardon or redemption. On his deathbed, Keeaumoku, father of Kaʻahumanu, warned Kamehameha: "Hookahi no kipi nui i koe o ko Aupuni, o ko wahine, a nui ko malama i ko wahine, paa ko Aupuni (The single threat to your rule is your wahine. Care for her and your kingdom will be secure)" ("Ka Moolelo o Na Kamehameha").

According to volume two of *Nānā I Ke Kumu: Look to the Source*:

> The capacity for mercy surely was recognized
> in the designation of certain chiefly persons as
> *puʻuhonua* or 'persons of refuge.' The *puʻuhonua*
> enclosures or 'places of refuge' where losing
> warrior or peacetime culprit could flee to and
> be safe are well known. But one might also
> run to a *puʻuhonua* person, and there be safe,
> forgiven, and freed from the punishment or
> vengeance of others. This *puʻuhonua* was always
> *aliʻi*. Kaʻahumanu, wife of Kamehameha, was
> such a person of refuge.

Shapeshifters banned, censored, or otherwise shit-listed, aka chosen family poem
Maʻi denotes genitals and biological genealogies.

Mai is a directional that signals movement toward the speaker.

"Mai, mai, e ʻai" is a common expression used to invite people to come and eat.

Hāʻōʻū is located on the east side of Maui, where my aunties and grandmother still keep a home. My paternal family continues to teach me about our genealogical history with this ʻāina.

Mahalo

"Maunakea" is dedicated to the kiaʻi, aloha ʻāina, and ʻai pōhaku wāhine who stand for their mountains and protect their waters. Kū kiaʻi mauna.

"So sacred, so queer" no kuʻu wai ʻapo Luseane Veisinia Moalapauʻu Raass.

"For sisters who pray with fire" is for my sister Kaimalie Revilla.

"The opposite of dispossession is not possession; it is connection" is for my cousins Kyla Siangco and Meagan Lau.

"The ea of enough" could not be written without the mentorship of Haunani-Kay Trask; it is for my nieces Tilipue, Kalaukoa & Lilikoikaʻehukai.

. . .

Aloha to the editors of the following journals and anthologies where some of these poems have appeared in different versions:

> "Basket," *The Missing Slate*
>
> "Eggs," *Sierra Magazine*
>
> "Getting ready for work," *Say Throne*, Tinfish Press
>
> "Iwi hilo means thigh bone means core of one's being"
> *Omniverse,* winner of Omnidawn 2021 Single Poem
> Broadside Poetry Contest
>
> "Kino," *Poetry*

"Lessons in quarantine" and "Maunakea," *Love in the Time of Covid: A Chronicle of a Pandemic*

"Memory as missionary position" and "After she leaves you, femme," *Literary Hub*

"Myth bitch," *ANMLY*, special folio on Queer Indigenous Poetics

"Preparing Kaʻuiki," *Nat. Brut*

"Shapeshifters banned, censored, or otherwise shit-listed, aka chosen family poem," *Living Nations, Living Words: An Anthology of First Peoples Poetry*

. . .

With humility and gratitude, I share aloha for the lands and waters, for the families, bio and chosen, for Haumea, Moʻoinanea, Hauwahine and all other moʻo who made it possible for me to love and create fearlessly.

To Maui, where I was born and raised; to Oʻahu, where I shed the most skin and found my chosen family; to the kai and muliwai of Hāna Bay and Kōkī; to the surf at Launiupoko, Barbers, and Waikīkī; to the Poʻolipilipi of Kalihi uka; to the Līlīlehua rains of Waiʻehu and Pālolo, you fed and nourished me.

To my wife Luseane, I will earn you every day. Mahalo for teaching me how to respect silence and its slow worldbuilding. I marvel at the mana of your hands, which are literally building our way to a home that gathers and protects. More slow dancing, more Sunday kind of loving, please.

To my sister Kai, I believe you and will always have your back. There is nothing in this multiverse like our sisterhood. To Kyla and Meagan, our bond makes me strong. To my kupunahine Lāʻieikawai, you are the source.

To my aunties who raised me on Maui, your resilience and laughter taught me how to choose abundance rather than fear. To Tataita, I believe in your art. When you were born, all I wanted to do was hold you and read to you. To my parents, John and Debbie, I love you both for the gifts you passed on to me, for making sure I knew I was loved every day.

Bryan, you've been seeing my mo'o, and without judgment you stayed and loved me. You even took portraits of these skins, making me feel seen in ways I didn't think I deserved. And oh the malu of mo'o and bear! Anjoli, for every new mo'o cave I called home, you were there with a car and a bottle of red wine. Important vulnerabilities found a voice with you in ride-or-die Pālolo living rooms and Kaka'ako hills. Thank you for the trust we cultivate together, for our radical lessons in letting shit go. CJ, the day my body broke into a million pieces, you drove out to Kailua and filled my arms with flowers, food, and other beautiful things. You told me I deserved protection, and once a friend loves you like that, there is no going back. Joce, you are my collaboration soulmate, my gut house sister, and damn it if you don't keep teaching me how to show the fuck up for what you really want. Mahalo for sharing your art, kino, and vision with this wao akua cover. Lyz, for your front porch and kitchen, where our talks about poetry and poetics grew wildly; Rajiv, for your generosity and fire—I submitted this manuscript because you believed in me; Aiko, you are decolonial love; Julia, for showing me the pleasure of being out and gay as fuck, talking shit like it was medicine, and "funny kine" adventures; Joy, for taking me to church and making art that I get to hang in my home and say "my friend made that"; Kim, for laughing, dancing & d.g. hour; Momi, for Whitney Houston healing, book shares, and loyal-as-fuck femme sisterhood; Aata, for sanctuary that summer in Mānoa and Waiāhole; Lee, your singing is hope and beauty; Kely James, for all the years no one could touch us; Māhealani and Kahala, for mo'oholic intersectionality; Grace, for our sisterhood and the ways your expansiveness makes me imagine better; Keali'i, for our poetry salons; Heoli, look what still grew; Hāwane, for your oli in

Pālolo and Karlsruhe; D. Kūhiō, for every exquisite corpse; ʻIlima and Presley, for inviting me to teach a poetry workshop on the first day at Puʻuhuluhulu; ʻIhilani and Bella, we stay!

Mahalo to Haunani-Kay Trask, for teaching me how to choose a "slyly / reproductive" life, for bringing me home to our country and keeping me home; kuʻualoha hoʻomanawanui, for telling me to go to grad school; Brandy Nālani McDougall, for knowing what we know and teaching me how to write through it honestly; Marie Alohalani Brown, for your moʻo knowledge and our moʻo pilina; Craig Santos Perez, for asking hard and beautiful questions about my poetics, our weekly calls during my dissertation, and years of brilliant mentorship; Cristina Bacchilega, for splendorousness and wonder; Cindy Franklin, for bringing Audre Lorde and Cherríe Moraga into my life; Robert Sullivan, for telling me I was a poet and asking the blunt question of my early poems—"where is *your* culture?" To Teresia Teaiwa, Noenoe Silva, Noelani Goodyear-Kaʻōpua, Allison Adelle Hedge Coke, Craig Howes, Laura Lyons, John Zuern, Kathy Ferguson, Susan Schultz, Brenda Shaughnessy, Natalie Diaz, Joy Harjo, Angela Peñaredondo, Abraham Mokunui (Kamehameha), Charlotte Boteilho (Baldwin), Mrs. Felipe (Maui Waena), and Mrs. Balicanta (Lihikai), mahalo for your work, patience, and guidance.

Rick Barot, mahalo for believing in the manuscript and seeing survivance in these skins. To the Milkweed ʻohana—especially Daniel Slager, Meilina Dalit, Claire Laine, Bailey Hutchinson, Mary Austin Speaker, Hadara Bar-Nadav, Yanna R. Demkiewicz, Shannon Blackmer, Tijqua Daiker, and Katie Hill—thank you for caring for these poems with tenderness and listening.

And for you, dear reader, mahalo for making story with me.

me ka naʻau haʻahaʻa

Bryan Kamaoli Kuwada

NOʻU REVILLA is an ʻŌiwi (Hawaiian) poet, performer, and educator. Her work has been featured in *Poetry*, Literary Hub, *ANMLY*, *Beloit Poetry Journal*, the Honolulu Museum of Art, and the Library of Congress. Born and raised in Waiʻehu on the island of Maui, she currently lives and loves in the valley of Pālolo on the island of Oʻahu, where she teaches creative writing with an emphasis on ʻŌiwi literature, spoken word, and decolonial poetics. She is an Assistant Professor at the University of Hawaiʻi-Mānoa.

milkweed
editions

Founded as a nonprofit organization in 1980, Milkweed Editions is an independent publisher. Our mission is to identify, nurture, and publish transformative literature, and build an engaged community around it.

Milkweed Editions is based in Bdé Óta Othúŋwe (Minneapolis) within Mní Sota Makhóčhe, the traditional homeland of the Dakhóta people. Residing here since time immemorial, Dakhóta people still call Mní Sota Makhóčhe home, with four federally recognized Dakhóta nations and many more Dakhóta people residing in what is now the state of Minnesota. Due to continued legacies of colonization, genocide, and forced removal, generations of Dakhóta people remain disenfranchised from their traditional homeland. Presently, Mní Sota Makhóčhe has become a refuge and home for many Indigenous nations and peoples, including seven federally recognized Ojibwe nations. We humbly encourage our readers to reflect upon the historical legacies held in the lands they occupy.

milkweed.org

Interior design by Tijqua Daiker and Mary Austin Speaker
Typeset in Athelas

Designed by Veronika Burian and José Scaglione, Athelas was
designed as part of the unique and diverse TypeTogether catalogue.
Established in 2006, TypeTogether sought to create innovative and
stylish solutions for the global professional typography market.
Spanning many languages and scripts, TypeTogether's catalogue is
internationally honored for its high quality as well as its personality.

Milkweed Editions, an independent nonprofit publisher, gratefully acknowledges sustaining support from our Board of Directors; the Alan B. Slifka Foundation and its president, Riva Ariella Ritvo-Slifka; the Amazon Literary Partnership; the Ballard Spahr Foundation; *Copper Nickel*; the McKnight Foundation; the National Endowment for the Arts; the National Poetry Series; the Target Foundation; and other generous contributions from foundations, corporations, and individuals. Also, this activity is made possible by the voters of Minnesota through a Minnesota State Arts Board Operating Support grant, thanks to a legislative appropriation from the arts and cultural heritage fund. For a full listing of Milkweed Editions supporters, please visit milkweed.org.